# Table of Contents

# Glossary

**Analogy**. A way of comparing things to show how they relate.

**Classifying**. Putting similar things into categories.

**Combining Form**. A word or word base used in forming words, such as **tele-** in telephone.

**Context**. A way to figure out the meaning of a new word by relating it to the words around it.

**Fact**. Information that can be proved. Example: Hawaii is a state.

**Generalization**. A statement or rule that applies to many situations or examples.

**Homographs**. Words that have the same spelling but different meanings.

**Idioms**. A phrase that says one thing but actually means something quite different.

**Inference**. Using logic to figure out what is unspoken but evident.

**Main Idea**. Finding the most important points.

**Metaphor**. An implied comparison of two unlike things. The words **like** and **as** are **not** used.

**Opinion**. Information that tells what someone thinks. It cannot be proved.

**Outline**. A chart containing the main ideas and important details of a reading selection.

**Paraphrase**. To restate a writer's ideas in your own words.

**Prefix**. One or more syllables at the beginning of a word that changes its meaning.

**Scan**. Looking for certain words in a reading selection to locate facts or answer questions.

**Sequencing**. Putting things in logical order.

**Similes**. Comparing two things that have something in common but are really very different. The words **like** and **as** are used in similes.

**Skim**. Reading quickly to get a general idea of what a reading selection is about.

**Suffix**. One or more syllables at the end of a word that changes its meaning. A suffix usually changes a word into a different part of speech, such as a verb into a noun. For example: assist to assistance.

**Summarize**. To write in your own words the most important ideas of a reading selection.

**Syllable**. Word divisions. Each syllable has one vowel sound.

**Syllabication**. Dividing words into parts, each with a vowel sound.

Name: 100

# Changing The Meanings Of Words

**Directions:** Add the prefixes to the root words to make new words. One is done for you.

| PREFIX | (MEANING) | ROOT WORD | NEW WORD |
|--------|-----------|-----------|----------|
| pre- | (before) | caution | precaution |
| | | historic | prehistoric |
| mid- | (middle) | night | midnight |
| | | stream | midstreem |
| post- | (after) | graduate | post graduate |
| | | war | post war |

**Directions:** Using the meanings in parentheses, complete each sentence with one of the words you just formed. One is done for you.

1. The dog howled at the moon at _____midnight_____. (middle of the night, 12 o'clock)

2. You must take every __precaution__ when working with chemicals. (care taken in advance)

3. She plans to do __post graduate__ work in medicine. (a course of study after graduation)

4. The dinosaur was the biggest ___pre historic___ animal. (the time before recorded history)

5. While wading, he lost his shoe __midstreem__. (in the middle of a stream)

6. The country made great progress during the early __post war__ years. (after a war)

Ⓛ

Name: _____

# Prefixes

**Directions:** Read the meanings of the following prefixes. Add a prefix to each word in the word box to make a new word that makes sense in each sentence below. Use the meanings in parentheses to help.

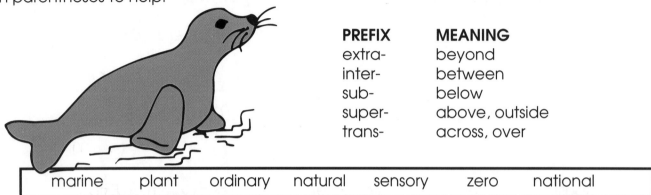

| PREFIX | MEANING |
|--------|---------|
| extra- | beyond |
| inter- | between |
| sub- | below |
| super- | above, outside |
| trans- | across, over |

| marine | plant | ordinary | natural | sensory | zero | national |
|--------|-------|----------|---------|---------|------|----------|

1. We're planning to _____*trans plant*_____ the lilac bush from our

front yard into our back yard. (move over from one place and plant in another)

2. The book was translated and became an _____*international*_____

best seller. (between or among nations)

3. Few animals can survive the

_____*sub zero*_____

temperatures in Antarctica. (below zero)

4. The _____*submarine*____dove deep to

avoid enemy fire. (a sailing vessel that can operate beneath the water)

5. He made an _____*extra ordinary*____effort to win the race. (beyond the ordinary)

6. The empty chair moved, apparently guided by some _____*supernatural*_____

force. (occuring outside the known forces of nature)

Name: _____

# Combining Forms

**Directions:** Read the meanings of the combining forms. After each sentence, write the meaning for the bold word. Use a dictionary if you need further help. One is done for you.

| FORM | MEANING |
|------|---------|
| uni- | one, single |
| bi- | two |
| tri- | three |
| quad- | four |
| octo- | eight |
| dec- | ten |
| centi- | hundred |

1. Do you believe the **unicorn** every truly existed?

   A mythical animal with one horn.

2. It took a **decade** for the oak tree to grow as tall as our house.

   A ten year period.

3. On our math test, we had to find the area of a **quadrangle**.

   A shape with for sides

4. The **centipede** scurried under the refrigerator when the kitchen light was turned on.

   insect 100 legs

5. The three streets come together to form a **triangle** around our farm.

   A shap with 3 sides

6. An **octopus** is a most unusual-looking animal!

   A sea animal with 8 legs.

Name: _____

# The Suffixes -ance And -ous

Suffixes are often used to change a word to a different part of speech, such as from a verb to a noun or from a noun to an adjective. The suffix **-ance** means "the condition or state of being"; **-ous** means "characterized by."

**Directions:** Add one of the suffixes to the word in parentheses to form a new word that makes sense in the sentence. One is done for you.

1. Mary was very (nerve) ___nervous___ the night before

   she starred in the class play.

2. The foolish young man spent all of his (inherit)

   __inheritance__ on a car.

3. The girl's (resemble) __resemblance__ to her mother is amazing.

4. A (mystery) __mysteryous__ woman in black entered the room but said nothing.

5. Tonight is the final (perform) __performance__ of the opera.

6. Jimmy told the most (outrage) __outrageous__ story about why he didn't

   have his homework.

7. The Grand Canyon is a (marvel) __marvelous__ sight.

8. The marriage of Joyce and Ted was a (joy) __joyous__

   occasion.

9. I am going to use my (allow) __allowance__

   to buy a Mother's Day gift.

10. The colonists who first settled in America were very (courage)

   __courageous__ people.

Name: _____

# The Suffixes -an, -ian, -ship

The suffixes **-an** and **-ian** mean "belonging to or living in" and the suffix **-ship** means "the quality of or having the office of".

**Directions:** Combine the suffix and the root word to form a new word.

| ROOT WORD | SUFFIX | NEW WORD | ROOT WORD | SUFFIX | NEW WORD |
|-----------|--------|----------|-----------|--------|----------|
| magic | -ian | magician | music | -ian | musician |
| America | -an | American | Europe | -an | European |
| friend | -ship | friendship | leader | -ship | leadership |

**Directions:** Use each of the words you just formed to complete one of the sentences. Then write another sentence using the word.

1. The _European_ settlers often came to America to escape persecution in their

   home countries. _I have a European friend._

2. The _magician_ drew gasps from the audience as he began to saw the woman in

   half. _The magician mad a helacopter disappear_

3. Dr. Mathews hopes that his new position on the school board will help him to assume a

   _leadership_ role in the community.

   _There is no leadership in the club._

5. Over the many years they knew each other, their _friendship_ remained strong.

   _Their friendship lasted forever._

6. After many years of practicing the piano daily, she has become a fine _musician_.

   _The musician became deaf._

7. All _American_ citizens should exercise their right to vote.

   _I am an American traveling to_ ~~the~~ _Scotland._

Name: _____

# Suffixes

The suffix **-ism** means "the condition of being" or "having the characteristics of." The suffix **-ist** means "one who does or is skilled at something."

**Directions:** Combine the suffix and root word to form a new word. Use the new word in a sentence.

1. national     +   ism: _____

_____

2. patriot     +   ism: _____

_____

3. alcohol     +   ism: _____

_____

4. criticize     +   ism: _____

_____

5. archaeology +   ist: _____

_____

6. violin     +   ist: _____

_____

7. terror     +   ist: _____

_____

8. chemistry     +   ist: _____

_____

9. piano     +   ist: _____

_____

Name: _____

# Review

**Directions:** Add one of the prefixes, suffixes, or combining forms to a word in the word box to complete each of the sentences. Use the definition in parentheses for a clue.

-ian   -ous   -ship   -an   -ist   extra-   trans-   pre-   micro-   super-

friend   music   geology   sensory   America   paid   wave   market   atlantic   danger

1. The _____ has a huge selection of fruits and vegetables. (a large food store)

2. The first_____ flight was a remarkable feat in the history of aviation. (across the Atlantic Ocean)

3. The woman claimed that she knew the future because of her _____ capabilities. (beyond the normal senses)

4. When mailing your payment, please use the _____ envelope. (paid in advance)

5. Mrs. Johnson studied the violin for many years to become the accomplished _____ she is today. (person skilled at music)

6. The _____ oven is a modern-day convenience. (operating with extremely small electo-magnetic waves)

7. Lightning is the most_____ part of a storm. (characterized by danger)

8. They raised the _____ flag over their campground in a gesture of patriotism. (belonging to America)

9. The Native Americans would often smoke a peace pipe as a sign of _____ . (the state of being friends

10. Dr. Stokes is the finest _____ at the university. (one who is skilled at geology, the study of the earth's crust)

# Homographs

A homograph has the same spelling as another word, but a different meaning.

**Directions:** Write the definition from the box for the bold word in each sentence.

| con' tract | *n.* | an agreement to do something |
|---|---|---|
| con tract' | *v.* | reduce in size, shrink |
| des' ert | *n.* | dry land that can support little plant and animal life |
| de sert' | *v.* | to abandon |
| Po' lish | *adj.* | of or belonging to Poland |
| pol' ish | *v.* | smooth and brighten by rubbing |
| proj' ect | *n.* | a proposal or undertaking |
| pro ject' | *v.* | to send forth in thoughts or imagination |

1. The **desert** seems to come to life in the evening, when the animals come out in search of food.

_____

2. You will have to sign a **contract** before I can begin work on your house.

_____

3. Iron is one of the metals that **contracts** as it cools.

_____

4. I hope you will not **desert** your friends now that they really need your support.

_____

5. She will **polish** the stone and then use it to make a necklace.

_____

6. The **Polish** people have been courageous in their struggle for freedom.

_____

7. **Project** yourself into the world of tomorrow with this amazing invention!

_____

8. I started this **project** on Monday, but it may be weeks before I finish it.

_____

# Homographs

**Directions:** After each sentence, write the meaning of the bold word. Write another sentence using a homograph for the word.

1. The owner of the pet store tied a bright red **bow** around each of the puppies' necks.

Meaning: _____

Sentence:_____

2. Today, fewer pipes are made from **lead**.

Meaning: _____

Sentence:_____

3. Marcia's new house is very **close** to ours.

Meaning: _____

Sentence:_____

4. Please **record** the time and day that we finished the project.

Meaning: _____

Sentence:_____

5. It takes only a **minute** to fasten your seatbelt, but it can save your life.

Meaning: _____

Sentence:_____

6. I cannot **subject** the animal to that kind of treatment.

Meaning: _____

Sentence:_____

Name: _____

# Words With Multiple Meanings

**Directions:** Read each sentence, then write another sentence using a different meaning for the bold word.

1. The prince will **succeed** his mother as ruler of the country.

_____

2. All through the National Anthem, Johnny was singing in the wrong **key**.

_____

3. There has been only a **trace** of rain this month.

_____

4. I can't get involved in a **cause** that I don't really believe in.

_____

5. It is very important to get plenty of **iron** in your diet.

_____

6. A police officer can **issue** a warning to those disturbing the peace.

_____

7. There is a mayoral candidate from each of the major political **parties**.

_____

8. You can take that **stack** of newspapers to be recycled.

_____

9. The judge will likely **sentence** the offender to a year in prison.

_____

10. The lawyer made a **motion** to have the charges dropped.

_____

Name: _____

# Metaphors And Similes

**metaphor** is an implied comparison of two unlike things.
**nilies** use **like** or **as** to compare two things.

**ections:** Underline the metaphor in the following sentences.
write the sentence using a simile.

She is a playful child, a real kitten!

_____

Life today is a merry-go-round.

_____

His emotions were waves washing over him.

_____

His childhood was an image in a rearview mirror.

_____

**rections:** Tell what is meant by the following sentences.

His mind was as changeable as spring weather.

_____

His demand was like a clap of thunder.

_____

Their was joy written on the children's faces on Christmas morning.

_____

13

Name: _____

# Idioms

An **idiom** is a phrase that says one thing but actually means something quite different.
**Example:** Now that's <u>a horse of a different color</u>!

**Directions:** Write the letter of the correct meaning for the bold words in each sentence.
One is done for you.

| |
|---|
| **a.** forgive and make up      **f.** pressed tightly together<br>**b.** fact kept secret for fear of disgrace    **g.** relatives and ancestors<br>**c.** something that dampens excitement    **h.** rudely ignored<br>**d.** get acquainted, become less formal    **i.** excessive paperwork<br>**e.** treat like royalty                      **j.** people were gossiping |

__g__ 1. There is a pirate and a president in our **family tree**.

_____ 2. The Johnsons went through a lot of **red tape** to adopt their baby.

_____ 3. Sophia **gave me the cold shoulder** when I tried to talk to her this morning.

_____ 4. The big homework assignment threw a **wet blanket** over my plans for an exciting weekend.

_____ 5. At a party, Judy likes to **break the ice** by having her guests play games.

_____ 6. **Tongues were wagging** when the principal called Chet into his office.

_____ 7. There were five people **sandwiched** into the back of the car.

_____ 8. She viewed her poor background as **a skeleton in her closet.**

_____ 9. Let's forget our past mistakes and **bury the hatchet**.

_____ 10. When the mayor came to visit our school, we **rolled out the red carpet.**

Name: _____

# Connotations And Denotations

A **connotation** is an idea suggested by or associated with a word or phrase. A **denotation** is the direct, explicit meaning of a word. **Example**: A connotation of mother is love. **Example**: A denotation of mother is parent.

**Directions:** The words in each group have a similar denotation, but one word has a connotation that suggests a negative feeling or idea. Circle the word with the negative connotation. One is done for you.

1. (stun)
   amaze
   astound

4. mischievous
   playful
   unruly

2. embarrassed
   ashamed
   blushing

5. dirty
   filthy
   soiled

3. chat
   discuss
   gossip

6. small
   puny
   miniature

7. abandon
   leave
   depart

**Directions:** Write the word whose connotation best fits the sentence.

1. Because he has had the flu for a few days, Mike's face looks very _____.
   (ghostly, pale, bloodless)

2. We will have to _____ the amount of food we waste.
   (shorten, shrink, reduce)

3. Did you get a good _____ from your former employer?
   (reference, mention, indication)

4. There was an _____ of measles at our school.
   (explosion, occurrence, outbreak)

Name: _____

# Review

**Directions:** Circle the word or phrase that best defines the bold words in each sentence.

1. What is the **subject** of the report your are writing for class?
   to cause to undergo
   topic
   course of study

2. Will you be going to the same **resort** where you spent your vacation last year?
   turn to for use or help
   to sort again
   place for rest and relaxation

3. They **rolled out the red carpet** for the contest winners.
   unrolled carpeting
   treated like royalty
   showed appreciation for

4. Mitch's past as a prisoner was **a skeleton in his closet**.
   fact kept secret for fear of disgrace
   dead person
   ancestor

5. Sally decided to **bury the hatchet**, and called her sister to apologize.
   say she was sorry
   forget past mistakes and make up
   go hunting

**Directions:** Circle the word that has the most positive connotation.

6. chat
   debate
   gossip

7. mischievous
   playful
   unruly

**Directions:** Underline the simile or metaphor in each of the following.

8. The clouds looked like cotton candy floating overhead.

9. Tina's nose was bent out of shape when she was not elected to the school council.

10. The flute on that record sounds like a rusty gate.

Name: _____

# Classifying

**Directions:** Write a category name for each group of words.

1. accordion  clarinet  trumpet      _____

2. wasp  bumblebee  mosquito      _____

3. antique  elderly  prehistoric      _____

4. chemist  astronomer  geologist  _____

5. nest  cocoon    burrow      _____

**Directions:** In each row, draw an X through the word that does not belong. Then write a sentence telling why it does not belong.

1. encyclopedia  atlas    novel    dictionary

_____

2. bass    otter    tuna    trout

_____

3. sister    grandmother    niece    uncle

_____

4. bark    beech    dogwood    spruce

_____

5. pebble    gravel    boulder    cement

_____

6. spaniel    Siamese    collie    doberman

_____

Name: _____

# Analogies

**Directions:** Choose the correct word from the word box to complete each one of the following analogies. One is done for you.

*Note:* **nose : smell :: tongue : taste** is simply another way of expressing an analogy.

| positive | wires | flower | tape | descend | drink | commercial | |
|----------|-------|--------|------|---------|-------|------------|---|
| grape | house | mouth | rude | bill | melted | worker | four |

1. banana : peel :: walnut : _____shell_____

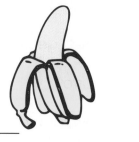

2. bird : beak :: duck : _____

3. up : ascend :: down : _____

4. cathedral : church :: mansion : _____

5. discourage : encourage :: negative : _____

6. nasal : nose :: oral : _____

7. prune : plum :: raisin : _____

8. hunger : eat :: thirst : _____

9. icicle : frozen :: water : _____

10. dandelion : weed :: lilac : _____

11. polite : impolite :: courteous : _____

12. plumber : pipes :: electrician : _____

13. employer : employee :: boss : _____

14. camera : film :: tape recorder : _____

15. triangle : three :: square : _____

16. newspaper : advertisement :: television : _____

Name: _____

# Fact Or Opinion?

A **fact** can be proved. An **opinion** cannot be proved.

**Directions:** Read the following sentences. Beside each one, write whether it is a fact or opinion. One is done for you.

_fact_ 1. All of the countries in South America are alike.

_____ 3. All South Americans are good swimmers.

_____ 2. People like the climate better in Peru than in Brazil.

_____ 1. The continent of South America is almost completely surrounded by water.

_____ 2. The only connection with another continent is a narrow strip of land, called the Isthmus of Panama, which links it to North America.

_____ 4. The Andes mountains run all the way down the western edge of the continent.

_____ 5. The Andes are the longest continuous mountain barrier in the world.

_____ 6. Geologists think the Andes are the most beautiful mountain range.

_____ 9. The Amazon River is the second longest river in the world — about 4000 miles long.

_____ 10. Half of the people in South America are Brazilians.

_____ 11. The United States of Brazil is bigger than the United States of America without Alaska.

_____ 12. Most South Americans want to live in Brazil.

_____ 13. Cape Horn is at the southern tip of South America.

_____ 14. The largest land animal in South America is the tapir, which reaches a length of six to eight feet.

Name: _____

# Cause And Effect

**Directions:** Read the paragraph. For each of the numbered sentences, circle the cause or causes and underline the effect or effects.

(1) All living things in the ocean are endangered by humans polluting the water. Pollution occurs in several ways. One way is the dumping of certain waste materials, such as garbage and sewage, into the ocean. (2) The decay bacteria that feed on the garbage use up much of the oxygen in the surrounding water, so other creatures in the area often don't get enough.

Other substances, such as radioactive waste materials, also can cause pollution. These materials often are placed in the water in securely sealed containers. (3) But after years of being exposed to the ocean water, the containers may begin to leak.

Oil is another major source of concern. (4) Oil is spilled into the ocean when tankers run aground and sink or when oil wells in the ocean cannot be capped. (5) The oil covers the gills of fish and causes them to smother. (6) Diving birds get the oil on their wings and are unable to fly. (7) When they clean themselves, they are often poisoned by the oil.

Rivers also can contribute to the pollution of oceans. Many rivers receive the runoff water from farmlands. (8) Fertilizers used on the farms may be carried to the ocean, where they cause a great increase in the amount of certain plants. Too much of some plants can actually be poisonous to fish.

Worse yet are the pesticides carried to the ocean. These chemicals slowly build up in shellfish and other small animals. These animals then pass the pesticides on to the larger animals that feed on them. (9) The build up of these chemicals in the animals can make them ill or cause their babies to be born deformed or dead.

Name: _____

# Review

**Directions:** Follow the directions for each section.

Add another word that belongs in each group. Write a category name for each group.

1. soccer  archery  skiing       _____    _____

2. Mercury  Pluto  Venus       _____    _____

3. miniature  shrimpy  dwarfed    _____    _____


Complete each analogy.

1. photograph : album :: _____ : _____.

2. gigantic : big :: _____ : _____.

3. fish : school :: _____ : _____.

Write **Fact** or **Opinion** to describe each sentence.

_____ 1. Hurricanes are also known as typhoons.

_____ 2. Hurricanes are the worst natural disasters.

_____ 3. All hurricanes begin over the ocean near the Equator.


**Directions:** Underline the cause and circle the effect. Write "true" if the cause and effect are appropriately related; write "no" if they are not.

_____ 1. While learning to ski, Jim broke his leg.

_____ 2. The river overflowed its banks and caused much damage.

_____ 3. The Cincinnati Reds won one hundred games last year so they probably will this year.

_____ 4. Because I started using a new toothpaste, all of the boys will be calling me for dates.

# Outlining

An **outline** contains the main ideas and important details of a reading selection. Making an outline is a good study aid. It is particularly useful when you must write a paper of your own.

**Directions:** Read the paragraphs, then use your own paper to finish the outline.

Weather has a lot to do with where animals live. Cold-blooded animals have body temperatures that change with the temperature of the environment. Cold-blooded animals include snakes, frogs, and lizards. They cannot live anywhere the temperatures stay below freezing for long periods of time. The body temperatures of warm-blooded animals do not depend on the environment. Any animal with hair or fur — including dogs, elephants, and whales — are warm-blooded. Warm-blooded animals can live anywhere in the world where there is enough food to sustain them.

Some warm-blooded animals live where snow covers the ground all winter. These animals have different ways to survive the cold weather. Certain animals store up food to last throughout the snowy season. For example, the tree squirrel may gather nuts to hide in his home. Other animals hibernate in the winter. The ground squirrel, for example, stays in its burrow all winter long, living off of the fat reserves on its body.

Title: _____

Main Topic: I. _____

Subtopic:　　A. Cold-blooded animals' temperatures change with environment

Detail:　　　　1. _____

Subtopic:　　B. _____

Detail:　　　　2. live anywhere there is food

Main Topic: II. _____

Subtopic:　　A. Animals have different ways to survive cold

Details:　　　　1. _____

　　　　　　　　2. _____

Name: _____

# Summarizing

A summary is a statement that includes all of the main ideas of a reading selection. To summarize, write in your own words the author's most important points.

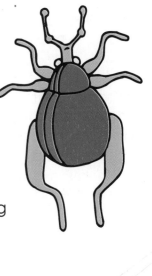

**Directions:** Read the paragraphs. Write a one sentence summary for each.

The boll weevil is a small beetle that is native to Mexico. It feeds inside the seed pods, or bolls, of cotton plants. The boll weevil crossed into Texas in the late 1800s. It has since spread into most of the cotton-growing areas of the United States. The boll weevil causes hundreds of millions of dollars worth of damage to cotton crops each year.

Summary: _____

_____

_____

Each spring, female boll weevils open the buds of young cotton plants with their snouts. They lay eggs inside the buds, and the eggs soon hatch into worm-like grubs. The grubs feed inside the buds, causing the buds to fall from the plant. They cut their way from one bud to another. Several generations of boll weevils may be produced in a single season.

Summary: _____

_____

_____

The coming of the boll weevil to the United States caused tremendous damage to cotton crops. Yet, there were some good results, too. Farmers were forced to plant other crops. In areas where a variety of crops were raised, the land is in better condition that it would have been if only cotton had been grown.

Summary: _____

_____

_____

Name: _____

# Making Generalizations

**Directions:** Read each paragraph, then circle the most appropriate generalization that covers the most examples.

Although many people think of reptiles as slimy, snakes and other reptiles are covered with scales that are dry to the touch. Scales are outgrowths of the animal's skin. Although in some species they are nearly invisible, in most they form a tile-like covering. The turtle's shell is made up of hardened scales that are fused together. The crocodile has a tough but more flexible covering.

Every reptile has hard scales.

The scales of all reptiles are alike.

All reptiles have scales.

The reptile's scales help to protect it from its enemies and conserve moisture in its body. Some kinds of lizards have fan-shaped scales that they can raise up to scare away other animals. They also can be used to court a mate. A reptile called the gecko can hang from a ceiling because of specialized scales on its feet. Some desert lizards have other kinds of scales on their feet that allow them to run over the loose sand.

Scales have many functions.

Scales scare away other animals.

Scales help reptiles adapt to their environments.

Snakes periodically shed their skins, leaving behind a thin impression of its body — scales and all. A lizard sheds its skin too, but it tears off in smaller pieces rather than in one big piece. Before it begins this process, which is called molting, the snake's eyes cloud over. The snake will go into hiding until they clear. When it comes out again, it brushes against rough surfaces to pull off the old skin.

Snakes go into hiding before they molt.

Reptiles periodically shed their skin.

A lizard's skin molts in smaller pieces.

Name: _____

# Paraphrasing

**Paraphrasing** means to put something into your own words.

**Directions:** Using synonyms and different word order, paraphrase the following paragraphs. The first one is done for you.

   Some of the earth's resources, such as oil and coal, can be used but once. We should always, therefore, be careful how we use them. Some materials that are made from natural resources, including metal, glass, and paper, can be re-used. This is called recycling.

Many natural resources, including coal and oil, can be used only one time. For this reason, it is necessary to use them wisely. There are other mate- rials made from resources of the earth that can be recycled, or used again. Materials that can be recycled include metal, glass, and paper.

   Recycling helps to conserve the limited resources of our land. For example, there are only small amounts of gold and silver ores in the earth. If we can recycle these metals, less of the ores need to be mined. While there is much more aluminum ore in the earth, recycling it is still important. It takes less fuel energy to recycle aluminum then it does to make the metal from ore. Therefore, recycling aluminum helps to conserve fuel.

_____

_____

_____

   It is impossible to get minerals and fossil fuels from the earth without causing damage to its surface. In the past, people did not think much about making these kinds of changes to the earth. They did not think about how these actions might affect the future. As a result, much of the land around mines was left useless and ugly. This is not necessary, because such land can be restored to its former beauty.

_____

_____

_____

Name: _____

# Skimming And Scanning

**Skimming** is reading quickly to get a general idea of what a reading selection is about. **Scanning** is looking for certain words to find facts or answer questions.

In skimming, look for headings and key words to give you an overall idea of what you are reading.

**Directions:** Quickly skim the paragraphs to answer this question:

1. What kind of time is used to describe the history of the earth?_____

   There are many different units to measure time. Probably the smallest unit that you use is the second, and the longest unit is the year. While a hundred years seems like a very long time to us, in the history of the earth, it is a smaller amount of time than one second is in a person's entire lifetime.

   To describe the history of the earth, scientists use geologic time. Even a million years is a fairly short period in geologic time. Much of the known history of the earth is described in terms of tens or even hundreds of millions of years. Scientists believe that our planet is about 4600 million years old. Since a thousand million is a billion, the earth can be said to be 4.6 billion years old.

**Directions:** Now scan the paragraph to find the answers to the following questions. When scanning, read the questions first, then look for specific words that will help you locate the answers. For example, for the first question, scan for the word "smallest."

1. For the average person, what is the smallest unit of time used? _____

2. In millions of years, how old do scientists believe the earth is?_____

3. How would you express that in billions of years?_____

Name: _____

# Colonists Come To America

After Christopher Columbus discovered America in 1492, many people wanted to come live in the new land. During the seventeenth and eighteenth centuries, a great many Europeans, especially the English, left their countries and settled along the Atlantic Coast of North America between Florida and Canada. Some came to make a better life for themselves. Others, particularly the Pilgrims, the Puritans, and the Quakers, came for religious freedom.

A group of men who wanted gold and other riches from the new land formed what they called the London Company. They asked the king of England for land in America and for permission to found a colony. They founded Jamestown, the first permanent English settlement in America, in 1607. They purchased ships and supplies, and located people who wanted to settle in America.

The voyage to America took about eight weeks and was very dangerous. Often fierce winds blew the wooden ships off course. Many were wrecked. The ships were crowded and dirty. Frequently passengers became ill, and some died. Once in America, the early settlers faced even more hardships. Much of the land was covered with dense forest.

**Directions:** Answer these questions about the colonists coming to America.

1. About how long did it take colonists to travel from England to America? _____

2. Name three groups that came to America to find religious freedom.

1) _____

2) _____

3) _____

3. Why was the London Company formed? _____

4. What was Jamestown? _____

# Early Colonial Homes

When the first colonists landed in America, they had to find shelter quickly. Their first homes were crude bark and mud huts, log cabins, or dugouts, which were simply caves dug into the hillsides. As soon as possible, the settlers sought to replace these temporary shelters with comfortable houses.

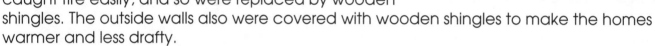

Until late in the seventeenth century, most of the colonial homes were simple in style. Almost all of the New England colonists — those settling in the northern areas or Massachusetts, Connecticut, Rhode Island, and New Hampshire — used wood in building their permanent homes. Some of the buildings had thatched roofs. However, they caught fire easily, and so were replaced by wooden shingles. The outside walls also were covered with wooden shingles to make the homes warmer and less drafty.

In the Middle Colonies — New York, Pennsylvania, New Jersey, and Delaware — the Dutch and German colonists often made brick or stone homes that were two-and-a-half or three-and-a-half stories high. Many Southern Colonists — those living in Virginia, Maryland, North Carolina, South Carolina, and Georgia — lived on large farms called plantations. Their homes usually were made of brick.

In the eighteenth century, some colonists became wealthy enough to replace their simple homes with mansions, often like those being built by the wealthy class in England. They were called "Georgian" houses because they were popular during the years that Kings George I, George II, and George III ruled England. Most were made of brick. They usually featured columns, ornately carved doors, and elaborate gardens.

**Directions:** Answer these questions about the homes of the colonists.

1. What were the earliest homes of the colonists?

_____

2. What were the advantages of using wooden shingles?

_____

3. What did Dutch and German colonists use to build their homes?

_____

4. What were the "Georgian" houses?

_____

# The Colonial Kitchen

The most important room in the home of a colonial family was the kitchen. Sometimes it was the only room.  And the most important element of the kitchen was the fireplace.  Fire was essential to the colonists, and they were careful to keep one burning at all times. Before the man of the house went to bed, he would make sure that the fire was carefully banked so it would burn all night. In the morning, he would blow the glowing embers into flame again with a bellows. If the fire went out, one of the children would be sent to a neighbor's for hot coals. Because there were no matches, it would sometimes take a half-hour to light a new fire using flint, steel, and tinder.

The colonial kitchen, quite naturally, was centered around the fireplace. One or two large iron broilers hung over the hot coals for cooking the family meals. Above the fireplace, a large musket and powder horn were kept for protection in the event of an attack and to hunt deer and other game. Also likely to be found near the fireplace was a butter churn, where cream from the family's cow was beaten until yellow flakes of butter appeared.

The furniture in the kitchen — usually benches, a table, and chairs — were made by the man or men in the family. It was very heavy and not very comfortable. The colonial family owned few eating utensils — no forks and only a few spoons, made of pewter, also by members of the family. The dishes included pewter plates, "trenchers" — wooden bowls with handles — and wooden mugs.

**Directions:** Read about an early colonial kitchen, then answer the questions.

1. What was the most important element of the colonial kitchen?_____

2. In colonial days, why was it important to keep a fire burning in the fireplace?

_____

3. Name two uses of the musket.

1)_____     2)_____

4. Who made most of the furniture in the early colonial home?_____

Name: _____

# Spinning

Most of the colonists could not afford to buy the clothes sent over from Europe. Instead, the women and girls, particularly in the New England Colonies, spent much time spinning thread and weaving cloth to make their own clothing. They raised sheep for wool and grew flax for linen.

In August, the flax was ready to be harvested and made into linen thread. The plants were pulled up and allowed to dry. Then the men pulled the seed pods from the stalks, bundled the stalks, and soaked them in a stream for about five days. The flax next had to be taken out, cleaned, and dried. To get the linen fibers from the tough bark and heavy wooden core, the stalks had to be pounded and crushed. Finally, the fibers were pulled through the teeth of a brush called a "hatchel" to comb out the short and broken fibers. The long fibers were spun into linen thread on a spinning wheel.

The spinning wheel was low, so a woman sat down to spin. First, she put flax in the hollow end of a slender stick, called the spindle, at one end of the spinning wheel. It was connected by a belt to a big wheel at the other end. The woman turned the wheel by stepping on a pedal. As it turned, the spindle also turned, twisting the flax into thread. The woman constantly dipped her fingers into water to moisten the flax and keep it from breaking. The linen thread came out through a hole in the side of the spindle. It was bleached and put away to be woven into pieces of cloth.

**Directions:** Number in order the steps to making linen thread from flax.

____ The woman sat at the spinning wheel and put flax in the spindle.

____ Seed pods were pulled from the stalks; stalks were bundled and soaked.

____ In August, the flax was ready to be harvested and made into thread.

____ The stalks were pounded and crushed to get the linen fibers.

____ The thread was bleached and put away to be woven into cloth.

____ The short fibers were separated out with a "hatchel."

____ The woman dipped her fingers into water to moisten the flax.

____ The long fibers were spun into linen thread on a spinning wheel.

____ The woman turned the wheel by stepping on a pedal, twisting the flax into thread.

____ The plants were pulled up and allowed to dry.

____ The linen thread came out through a hole in the side of the spindle.

Name: _____

# Review

**Directions:** Read the paragraph, then follow the directions.

According to one estimate, 75 percent of all fresh water on the earth is in the form of ice. The polar regions of the earth are almost completely covered by ice. In some places, the ice is more than 8000 feet thick. If all of this ice were spread out evenly, the earth would be covered with a 100-foot thick layer of ice. Although ice is not an important source of fresh water today, it could be in the future. Some people have proposed towing large, floating masses of ice to cities to help keep up with the demand for fresh water.

1. Complete the outline of the paragraph.

Title: _____

Main Topic: I.  75 percent of fresh water on earth is ice

Subtopics:  A. _____

B. _____

2. Summarize the paragraph by writing in your own words the most important ideas.

_____

3. Check the most appropriate generalization:
   ☐ Ice is the most plentiful source of fresh water
   ☐ Ice is important to the future

4. Paraphrase the paragraph by restating it in your own words.

_____

5. Is the author's purpose to inform, entertain, or persuade?_____

6. Where would you look to find information on the polar ice caps?_____

Name: _____

# Review

Many great colonists made an impact on American history. Among them was Benjamin Franklin, who left his mark as a printer, author, inventor, scientist, and statesman. He has been called "the wisest American."

Franklin was born in Boston in 1706, one of thirteen children in a very religious Puritan household. Although he had less than two years of formal education, his tremendous appetite for books served him well. At age twelve, he became an apprentice printer at *The New England Courant* and soon began writing articles that poked fun at Boston society.

In 1723, Franklin ran away to Philadelphia, where he started his own newspaper. He was very active in the Philadelphia community. He operated a book store and was named postmaster. He also helped to establish a library, a fire company, a college, an insurance company, and a hospital. The well-known *Poor Richard's Almanac* was first printed in 1732.

Over the years, Franklin maintained an interest in science and mechanics, leading to such inventions as a fireplace stove and bifocal lenses. In 1752, he gained world fame with his kite-and-key experiment, which proved that lightning was a form of electricity.

Franklin was an active supporter of the colonies throughout the Revolutionary War. He helped to write and was a signer of the Declaration of Independence in 1776. In his later years, he skillfully represented America in Europe, helping to work out a peace treaty with Great Britain.

**Directions:** Read about Benjamin Franklin, then answer the questions.

1. The main idea is:
   ☐ Many great colonists made an impact on American history.
   ☐ Benjamin Franklin was a great colonist who left his mark as a printer, author, inventor, scientist, and statesman.

2. How did Benjamin Franklin gain world fame? _____

_____

3. What important document did Franklin sign and help to write? _____

4. Number in order the following accomplishments of Benjamin Franklin:

____ Served as a representative of America in Europe.

____ Began printing *Poor Richard's Almanac.*

____ Experimented with electricity.

____ Started his own newspaper.

____ Helped to write and signed the Declaration of Independence.

____ Served as apprentice printer on *The New England Courant.*